A New True Book

INDIANS

Original story by Teri Martini

Edited by Margaret Friskey

This "true book" was prepared
under the direction of
Illa Podendorf,
formerly with the Laboratory School,
University of Chicago

 CHILDRENS PRESS, CHICAGO

Dancer at Apache powwow

PHOTO CREDITS

Carlton C. McAvey—Cover, 2, 4, 21 (2 photos), 22, 44 (2 photos)

Smithsonian Institution, National Anthropological Archives, Bureau of American Ethnology Collection—18, 19, 20 (left), 37

James P. Rowan—41

Reinhard Brucker—26 (3 photos), 28 (2 photos), 29, 32 (3 photos)

Bill Thomas—8

Lynn M. Stone—16

Tom Winter—25

Allan Roberts—10 (2 photos), 34

Harry & Pat Michalski—43 (right)

Historical Picture Service, Inc. Chicago—13, 15, 20 (right), 30, 36, 39 (2 photos), 40, 43 (left)

E
970
MAR

Library of Congress Cataloging in Publication Data

Martini, Teri.
  Indians.

  (A New true book)
  Revised edition of: The true book of Indians. 1954.
  Summary: Describes in simple text how the Indians of the seacoast, plains, deserts, swamps, and woodlands lived and how their way of life was influenced by the environment.
  1.   Indians of North America—Juvenile literature.   [1.   Indians of North America]
I.   Title.
E77.4.M28 1982   970.004'97   81-15442
ISBN 0-516-01628-8   AACR2

93-377

TABLE OF CONTENTS

COLUMBUS IN
THE NEW WORLD

When Columbus landed
in the New World, he
thought he was in India.
So he called the people
he met Indians. We still
call them Indians—
American Indians.

Later explorers and
settlers found Indian tribes
in all parts of America.

All Indians used wisely
what there was in the part
of the country that was
their home. So they lived
in very different ways.

INDIANS OF THE NORTHWEST COAST

These Indians carved their canoes from great logs in the forest nearby.

These Indians of the northwest coast built their houses of wood, too.

Totem pole at Ketchikan, Alaska

They carved tall tree trunks. These were totem poles. They told the stories of the tribe.

Much of their food came from the rivers.

Men and boys fished in the rivers that ran to the sea.

Nets and spears were fine for catching fish in the rivers.

But the sea was full of food, too.

Sometimes men went to sea in a big canoe. They went to catch a whale.

Now they took their harpoons with them.

Right: Stone carved pipes from Alaska
Below: Harpoon head dug up at a peat bog. The maple seed shows how big the harpoon head is.

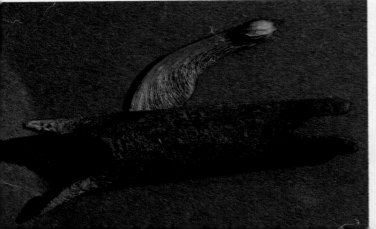

The strongest men threw harpoons at the whale.

Swish! Away went the whale, pulling the canoe through the water.

When, at last, the whale was dead, there was food for many days.

The people were proud of the brave fishermen.

Everyone helped cut up the whale. All the people got some of the meat.

The women and girls cleaned the meat with sharp shells.

They cooked some of it. This could be eaten right away.

Much of the meat was dried in smoke from the fire. This was packed away for winter use.

Papago Indian basket maker in Arizona. This photograph was taken in 1916.

The women made hats
and skirts and mats and
baskets from tree bark and
grasses. Little girls helped
them.

They used hair from the
dogs to make blankets.
Winter clothes were
made from animal skins.
A Northwest Coast
Indian liked to have a
giveaway party. This was
called a potlatch. He might
give away everything he
had, just to show how rich
he was.

The Potlatch, by Frederic Remington

There were gifts and
food for everyone. There
was singing and dancing
and racing on the sand.

INDIANS OF THE PLAINS

These Indians got almost everything they needed from the buffalo. They got
- food
- clothing
- skins for tepees
- hair for blankets
- bones for tools

Buffalo herd

They never killed more buffalo than they needed.

The women were busy after a hunt.

Hair from the buffalo's head was used for blankets. The furry hide made winter robes and moccasin soles.

Women scraped hair from the skins. Then they sewed the skins together to make tepees.

Many of the Plains Indians lived almost entirely on buffalo meat. Some of it was cut in strips and smoked over a fire. This meat was ground up and mixed with dried berries to make pemmican. This could be stored for winter use.

Arapaho camp near Fort Dodge, Kansas. Buffalo meat is drying in background.

Family of Stump Horn, a Cheyenne Indian, with a horse travois.
Do you see the two children in the travois basket?

When the buffalo moved, the whole tribe had to follow them. Everything a family needed was put on a wooden frame called a travois. This was pulled by a dog or horse.

The women cooked, cared for the children, and made the clothes. They sewed deerskin with bone needles.

Sometimes they made designs with beads or porcupine quills.

20

They spun yarn from buffalo hair and wove it into blankets.

A Plains Indian man spent his time hunting or fighting.

A warrior painted his face with colored clay. Each tribe had its own face-paint designs.

They fought with spears
or bows and arrows.

The important thing for a
warrior was to show that
he was brave.

Eagle feathers were
earned by acts of bravery.

A message could be sent a long way with smoke signals. A blanket was held over a fire. When it was lifted a puff of smoke rose. The number of puffs and the time between them had meaning.

Some Plains Indian tribes spoke different languages. When they met they had to talk a sign language with their hands.

INDIANS OF
THE SOUTHWEST

These Indians lived in
hot, dry, desert country.

They used clay and
grass to make sun-dried
bricks called adobe.

They built round brick
ovens where they cooked
most of their food.

Adobe houses

They used their bricks to build houses. They were four or five stories high. Ladders led from one story to the next.

Spaniards called these people Pueblo Indians. In Spanish, pueblo means village.

Above: Navajo rug
Above right: Woman weaving wool blanket
Right: Navajo sand painting

These Indians farmed
with pointed sticks and
hoes made of wood or
bone.

There was very little rain. Water for the plants had to be carried from a nearby stream. Some tribes dug ditches to carry water to the fields.

They raised corn and beans and squash.

The corn was dried on the hot, flat roofs. Some of the squash and beans were dried, too. The dried food would keep for a long time.

Above: Herding sheep in Monument Valley. The Spanish brought sheep to the Southwest. Right: Hopi corn kachina doll. Many Pueblo ceremonies were devoted to asking for rain so the corn would grow.

Indian women ground the dried corn between stones. They baked thin corn bread in their round brick ovens. They made corn dumplings and corn stew.

Rain god pottery
made by the
Tesuque Pueblo

Pueblo Indians were happy when it rained. Then they did not have to carry water to the fields. The crops were good.

These Indians thought that strange people living under the ground could make it rain.

One tribe, the Hopi, did a snake dance to bring rain. It lasted nine days. Then the snakes were put out on the desert. The Indians thought the snakes would tell the underground people to send rain.

Many Indian tribes had special dances.
This drawing shows a Sioux Indian war dance.

Wild cotton grew in the desert. The Pueblo Indians wove this into cloth. They made dresses, shirts, and skirts. They trimmed the edges with colored threads.

The Indians had leather boots to protect their feet from rocks and rough grasses.

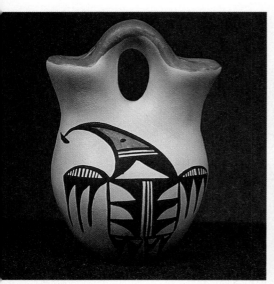

Above: Acoma Pueblo
marriage vase
Above right: Hopi pot
Right: Isleta Pueblo
pottery

The women made
beautiful clay jars. Some
were for water. Some were
for storing food.

INDIANS OF THE SOUTHEAST

Many settlers came to what is now Florida.

Some of the Indians fled back into the swamps. These were the Seminoles.

It was hard to farm where there was so much water. So these Indians learned to live on the wild plants and animals they found there.

Houses were built on posts to raise them off the damp ground. Wooden roofs were covered with leaves from the palm trees. It was so hot the houses had no walls.

Seminole Indian village in the Everglades

The Seminoles hunted deer and wild turkeys for food. They fished with nets and spears. They even knew how to catch fish with their hands.

They hunted brightly colored birds with blow guns. They liked to wear the beautiful feathers.

Choctaw Indians playing ball

They wore animal tails
for good luck.

These Indians liked ball
games.

In one game they threw
the ball back and forth
and caught it in a net.

INDIANS OF THE NORTHEAST WOODLANDS

Indians of the northeast woodlands made canoes of birchbark. They fished with nets and spears in the many lakes and rivers.

Chippewa Indian hunters in birchbark canoe, photographed about 1900.

They grew corn, beans, pumpkins, and sweet potatoes in their gardens. And the women also gathered grapes, nuts, and berries in the woods.

They tapped the maple trees for sap.

These Indians set traps in the woods for small animals. They hunted deer with bows and arrows.

Above: Inside a Cree home
Left: Earth lodge women

Sometimes the women roasted the meat over the fire. Sometimes they dropped it into a jar of water. Then they dropped in hot stones that made the water boil.

Iroquois longhouses

The Iroquois Indians built a longhouse of logs and bark. There were rooms on each side of a long hall. Twenty families could live in one longhouse.

The Delawares lived in round, one-room houses called wigwams. They were made of bent saplings covered with bark.

Wigwam

Woodlands Indians wore very little in the summertime. In winter they wore soft, warm clothes made of deerskin.

There was deep snow in the woods in winter. The Indians made snowshoes of wooden frames and strips of leather. These helped them walk over the snow.

Above: Indian masks on display at Prince
Rupert, British Columbia
Left: Mandan chief wearing ceremonial dress

The medicine men were busy in the spring and fall. They put on false faces—(masks). They went from house to house. They sang. They danced. They shook turtle-shell rattles. They thought they were chasing away the evil spirits that caused sickness.

Beads made from shells were called wampum. Sometimes these Indians wore them. They trimmed their clothes with them. They wove belts of them. Pictures on some strips were a record of a treaty. Strings of wampum were used for money.

No one knows how many hundreds of years Indians had lived in the New World before Columbus saw them. We do know that they loved the land and used wisely what it had to offer. The parts of the country were different. That is why they lived in such different ways.

We can learn much about taking care of the land from the Indians.

WORDS YOU SHOULD KNOW

birchbark(BERCH • bark) —the outer covering of the birch tree that peels off

blow gun(BLO • gun) —a tube through which an arrow or other object is blown

entire(en • TYRE) —complete; all

evil(EE • vil) —bad; wicked

explorer(x • PLOR • er) —a person who travels in places to discover new lands

harpoon(har • POON) —a spear with a rope attached to it

hide(HYDE) —the skin of an animal

palm(PAHM) —a type of tree that grows in warm climates

pemmican(PEM • ih • kin) —food made of smoked meat and berries

quill(KWILL) —sharp, hollow spine

sap —a liquid that flows through plants

sapling(SAP • ling) —a young tree

settler(SET • ler) —a person who moves into and lives in a new region

swamp —an area of soft and wet land full of mud

tap —to put a hole into a tree to drain liquid from it

tepee —a tent in the shape of a cone made of animal skins or bark

totem pole(TOE • tim POLE) —a post that is carved and painted to tell a story

travois(trav • OY) —a wooden frame like a sled, pulled by an animal, used for hauling things

treaty(TREE • tee) —an agreement made between two or more groups

tribe(TRYBE) —a group of people who live together

wampum(WAW • pum) —small beads made from shells and strung together into a necklace or belt

wigwam(WIG • wam) —a shelter made of animal skin or bark

INDEX

About the Author

Teri Martini is a teacher turned writer. Her titles in the True Book series grew out of specific needs she saw in her elementary school classrooms. She has a Masters Degree in education from Columbia University. Among the 22 books she has written, 14 are for children. Her short stories and articles have appeared in Scott Foresman Basic Readers, Childcraft, Scholastic Publications, and Teen Magazine. At present she divides her time between writing and teaching other writers to write for children through The Institute of Children's Literature in Redding Ridge, Connecticut. She is listed in Who's Who of American Women, Contemporary Authors *and* The International Dictionary of Biography.

The Children's Reading Institute offers several card learning programs for development of reading and math skills. For information write to Children's Reading Institute, Drawer 709, Higganum, CT 06441.